This book has been made with responsibly sourced uncoated paper (and love) and is suitable for colouring in using pens, pencils, or crayons of your choosing... so feel free to be as creative as you like!

**First published in 2024
by Crafty Birdie Designs**

Text copyright © Diana Gagic, 2024
Illustrations copyright © Diana Gagic, 2024

Design for print by
Form + Flow

Copy edited by
James Booth

Created in Yorkshire

The moral right of Diana Gagic to be identified as the author and illustrator of this work has been asserted in accordance with Sections 77 and 78 of the Copyright, Designs, and Patents Act 1988.

All rights reserved.
No part of this book may be reproduced, transmitted, or stored in any form or by any means, graphic, electronic, or mechanical, including photocopying, taping and recording, without prior written permission from the original publisher.

www.linktr.ee/craftybirdiedesigns

Printed in England

ISBN 978-1-9160072-9-1

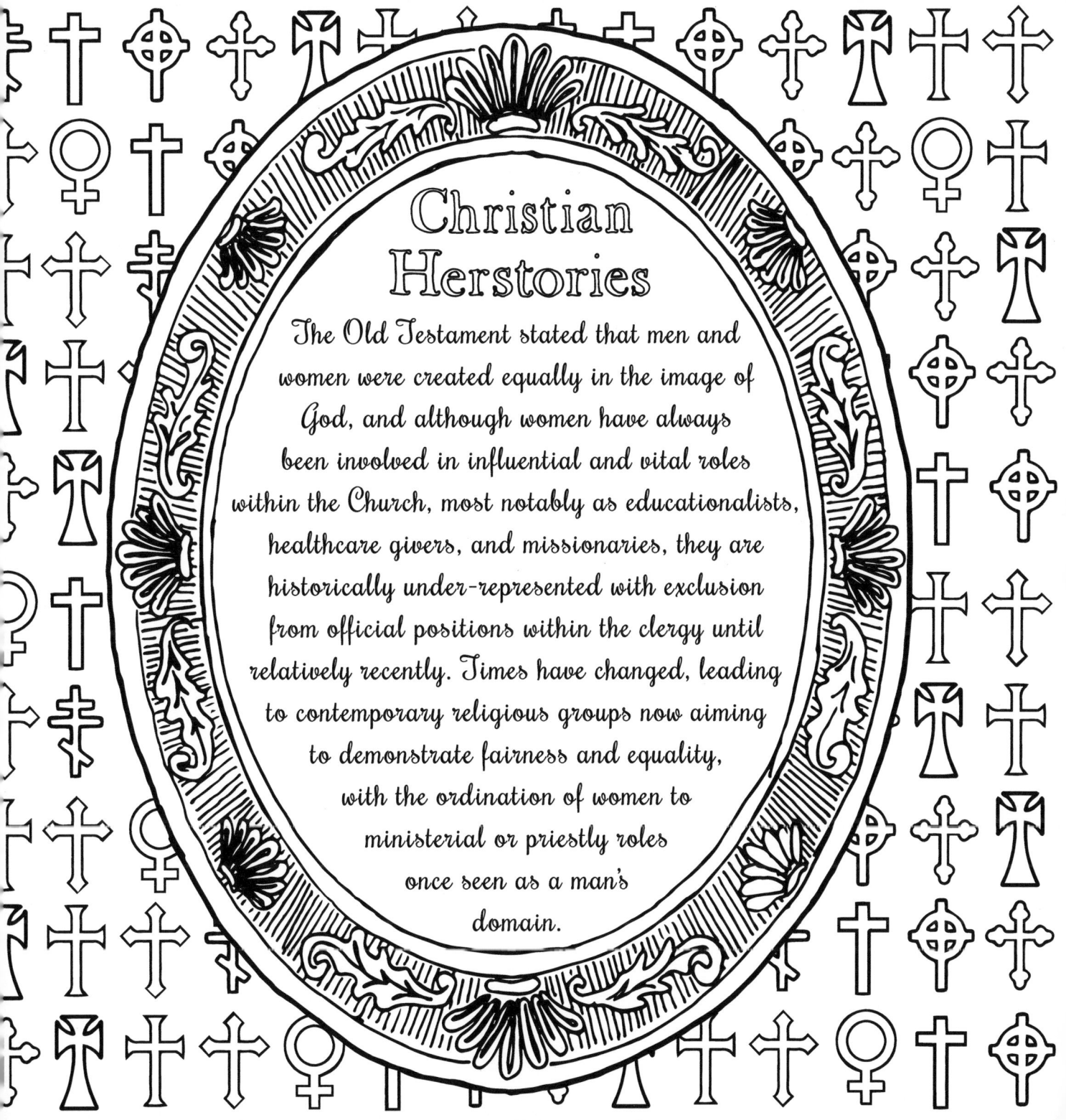

Christian Herstories

The Old Testament stated that men and women were created equally in the image of God, and although women have always been involved in influential and vital roles within the Church, most notably as educationalists, healthcare givers, and missionaries, they are historically under-represented with exclusion from official positions within the clergy until relatively recently. Times have changed, leading to contemporary religious groups now aiming to demonstrate fairness and equality, with the ordination of women to ministerial or priestly roles once seen as a man's domain.

Eve

Eve is considered the Mother of the human race in the Book of Genesis in the Hebrew Bible. The name Eve is commonly believed to mean "source of life." According to the origin story of the Abrahamic religions (Judaism, Christianity, and Islam), Adam and Eve were made by God on the sixth day as part of the original creation of life. Eve, unlike the rest of God's creations, was fashioned from a rib bone taken from Adam, to live side-by-side in powers, faculties, and rights. Adam was instructed to look after the Garden of Eden, free to eat from any tree in the garden except the Tree of the Knowledge of Good and Evil. Eve, tricked by a serpent's argument that eating the forbidden fruit would not harm but would bring benefits, shares the fruit with Adam, and God banishes both from the garden as punishment for defying his command. Christian churches differ on how they view Adam and Eve's disobedience to God, and to the consequences that those actions had on humanity. The Catholic Church by ancient tradition recognises Eve as a saint, alongside Adam, and the traditional religious feast of Saints Adam and Eve has been celebrated on 24th December since the Middle Ages.

Mary, Mother of Christ
(c. 18 BC - 33 AD)

Mary was a first-century woman of Nazareth, born into a devout Jewish family in Galilee when it was part of the ancient Roman Empire. The first Christians called Mary the Mother of God because she gave birth to Jesus, who comprises the Trinity, along with the Father and the Holy Spirit. Mary is considered by millions of faithful followers to be a central figure of Christianity, as the patron saint of all humanity, and is known by many names, including Our Lady, Queen of Angels, Mary of Sorrows, Queen of the Universe, Mother Mary, the Blessed Virgin, and Virgin Mary, in accordance with the belief of the Immaculate Conception and virgin birth of Jesus in a lowly stable in Bethlehem. In keeping with the faith, Jesus, the divine Son of God, died on the cross for the sins of our world, then resurrected and ascended into heaven. The Bible then mentions how, immersed in prayer, Mary receives the Holy Spirit together with the 12 disciples, and thus participates in the birth of the Church "let us be always open, as she was, to welcome the will and Spirit of God."

Phoebe
(1st Century)

Phoebe was a leader in the early Christian movement and was the only woman named as a deacon in the Bible. Phoebe, whose name means "pure", "radiant", or "bright" was from Cenchrea, a harbour in Corinth, Greece — it is thought probable that Phoebe had served as a minister in the church there. Ancient ruins and historical records show that Corinth contained many temples honouring the Greek mythological gods, and the port of Cenchrea had statues of Aphrodite (the goddess of love) and Poseidon (god of the sea) on its shore. This gives us an insight into the religious beliefs leading up to the time before the Roman Empire converted to Christianity in the 4th century AD. Phoebe played a vital role in spreading the new faith to Rome and is mentioned in the New Testament by the Apostle Paul in his Epistle to the Romans when she was assigned to deliver his letter. Paul introduced Phoebe as one of his most trusted patrons and emissaries and refers to her by the Greek term diakonos, which most Bibles translate as "deacon." Paul's high recommendation of Phoebe equates her with other male leaders who travelled to preach the holy gospel.

Agnes of Rome
(c. 291 - 304)

Agnes was born into Roman nobility, and legend has it that her beauty attracted a high-ranking suitor, who was insulted by her devotion to God and refusal to marry. Agnes was reported to the pagan authorities as a follower of Christianity, illegal in Rome at the time, and led to her execution at just thirteen. Venerated as a virgin martyr, Saint Agnes is the patron saint of young girls and chastity, and her name is included in the First Eucharistic Prayer. Since the Middle Ages, Saint Agnes has traditionally been depicted as a young girl with a lamb, representing her innocence and name, 'Agnus' being the Latin word for 'lamb'. Since the 16th century, a traditional blessing of the lambs is carried out on January 21st, the anniversary of her martyrdom. On the feast day of St Agnes, two lambs are brought from the Trappist abbey of Tre Fontane in Rome to be blessed by the Pope. In summer, their wool is shorn and used to weave vestments called pallia. Popes and metropolitan archbishops wear the 'pallium' as a sign of their union as 'shepherds' to the faithful within the Catholic Church.

Hilda of Whitby
(c. 614 - 680)

Hilda or 'Hild' of Whitby is one of the most revered abbesses from the early medieval period and is a crucial figure in the history of early Christianity. She was a Northumbrian princess who converted to Christianity with the rest of the court of her great-uncle, King Edwin of Deira when she was 13. Influenced by the teachings of the Irish monk Aidan, the Bishop of Lindisfarne, Hilda went on to found Streanaeshalch Monastery in Whitby in 657. There she taught justice, piety, chastity, peace, and charity to both monks and nuns and trained honorary priests and bishops. 'No one there was rich, and none poor, for they had all things common'. In 664 Hilda's monastery hosted the Synod of Whitby; a meeting which brought together the Celtic and Roman Christians to unify the date for the celebration of Easter, strengthening and furthering the growth of Christianity during a crucial, war-torn period of English history. Saint Bede chronicled her life of virtue and her much sought-after wisdom. She was a great supporter of the arts and music and is the patron saint of learning, culture, and poetry. On her deathbed, she urged her community "to preserve the gospel peace amongst themselves and towards all others."

Margaret of Scotland
(c. 1045 - 1093)

Margaret of Scotland, also known as Margaret of Wessex or fondly as The Pearl of Scotland, was an exiled English princess and a Scottish queen and is the patron saint of the poor and vulnerable of Scotland. Born in Hungary to the expatriate English prince Edward the Exile, Margaret and her family returned to England in 1057. Despite her devout religious leanings, Margaret felt compelled to marry Malcolm III Canmore, king of Scotland, and together had eight children. She was a key figure in the reform of the Scottish Church, successfully inviting the Benedictine Order to establish a monastery in Dunfermline, Fife in 1072 and established ferries to assist pilgrims journeying from south of the Firth of Forth to St Andrew's in Fife. Margaret was probably present at the laying of Durham Cathedral's foundation stone in 1093, in the same year, her husband and their eldest son were both killed in the Battle of Alnwick. Margaret is said to have died while praying just two days after hearing the tragic news and is buried at Dunfermline Abbey.

Hildegard of Bingen
(c. 1098 - 1179)

Hildegard of Bingen, also known as the Sibyl of the Rhine, was the Mother Superior of a German Benedictine convent who became legendary for her great and varied knowledge. At a time when few women could write, Hildegard became a respected theologian, philosopher, musician, mystic, visionary, preacher, poet, artist, writer, and healer. Considered the Medieval Mother of Science by many, with translations of her writings on natural science and holistic medicine still in use to this day. Way ahead of her time, she called for an awakening of 'greening power' in us to look after our world and advocated a balanced diet, sufficient rest, alleviation of stress, and a moral lifestyle. She is also one of the best-known, and most recorded composers of sacred monophony (single singer or instrument), with more surviving chants than any other composer from the entire Middle Ages. Hildegard attributed her outstanding creativity to spiritual visions, most notable in her illustrated works known as Scivias; a series of symbolic paintings and writings, showing the path to moral salvation. In a male-dominated church, she went on preaching tours, demonstrating how men and women are partners in God's work, and founded the monasteries of Rupertsberg in 1150 and Eibingen in 1165. She is also noted for the invention of a new language known as Lingua Ignota. Canonised as a Roman Catholic saint in 2012.

Paraskeva of the Balkans
(11th Century)

This Orthodox saint's proper name is Paraskeva of the Balkans, but she is also known as Saint Petka. Born to wealthy, landowning parents in Epivates on the shores of the Sea of Marmara, near present-day Istanbul, she claimed that God spoke to her directly as a child while in church— "Whoever wants to be my disciple must deny themselves and take up their cross and follow me." (Mark 8, 34). Her parents did not support her decision to follow a devoutly religious life, but these words inspired her to give her rich clothes away to the poor and to flee to Constantinople, to devote her life to God. Paraskeva was said to have lived at the church of the Most Holy Theotokos in Heraclea Pontica, Bithynia for 5 years. While there, she led an austere life, and experienced visions of the Virgin Mary, whom she claimed told her to visit Jerusalem, where she remained for several years, settled in a convent in the desert near the Jordan River. Paraskeva died at age 27 and was buried at the church of the Holy Apostles, Kallikrateia. Her remains were said to be found intact many years after burial and are still considered a holy destination of pilgrimage.

She is a patron to spinners, needleworkers, embroiderers, and weavers, and a feast day is celebrated in her honour on the 14th of October.

Elizabeth of Portugal
(1271-1336)

Elizabeth of Portugal, also known as the Peacemaker, Holy Queen, and Portuguese Santa Isabel de Portugal, was the daughter of King Peter III of Aragon and his wife Constance of Sicily. Elizabeth received a strict and pious education and became Queen Consort of Portugal in 1282, following her marriage to King Dinis of Portugal, historically considered to be a good ruler but an unfaithful husband. Despite the morally corrupt court life she found herself in, Elizabeth maintained a life of dignified piety and founded many charitable establishments to help the sick and the poor. She earned the title of Peacemaker on account of her ability to solve disputes and prevented a Civil War in 1323 when she rode between and reconciled the two armies when her son Afonso rebelled against his father. Following her husband's death in 1325, Elizabeth devoted the rest of her life to aiding the poor and the sick in a monastery that she had founded, now known as the Monastery of Santa Clara-a-Velha in Coimbra. She died following the exertions of her final peace-making act on the battlefield, this time between her son, then King Afonso IV, and Alfonso XI of Castile. She was canonised as a saint in 1625 by the Roman Catholic Church.

Julian of Norwich
(c. 1343 - 1416)

Julian of Norwich, also known as Juliana of Norwich, the Lady Julian, Dame Julian, or Mother Julian, was an English anchoress, Christian mystic, and theologian of the Middle Ages. An anchorite is someone who practiced extreme self-denial by staying permanently enclosed in one place for religious reasons. Her real birth name is uncertain, 'Julian' being the name of the church that she was anchored to, living in a small cell attached to St Julian's Church, Norwich. During one of the darkest periods of history, at the time of the Black Death and political unrest, it is said that the holy hermit Julian 'anchored the light of God on earth'. While self-entombed, with her cat for company, Julian is believed to have created the earliest surviving English language works by a woman, the Revelations of Divine Love. Her optimistic theology was based on her visions and spiritual revelations on the certainty of being loved by God and spoke of God's omnibenevolence. Female anchorites outnumbered their male counterparts, and the dissolution of the monasteries ordered by Henry VIII in the late 1530s brought the restrictive anchorite tradition to an end in England.

St Julian is known as the patron saint of contemplatives and cats.

Catherine of Siena
(1347 - 1380)

Caterina di Jacopo di Benincasa was born and raised in Siena, Tuscany, and from a young age, against the will of her parents, wanted to devote her life to God. She is known for being a mystic and went on to become one of only four women who were named Doctor of the Church, meaning that her extensive writings, including The Dialogue, her prayers, and political letters, hold special authority in Roman Catholicism. When Catherine was just 16, her older sister died, and their parents wanted her to marry her widower brother-in-law. Catherine was so strongly opposed to this, that she cut off her long hair in protest and joined the Mantellate Sisters; a group of pious women, primarily widows, living a life of prayer outside of a convent's walls. Her writings illustrate her belief in the "inner cell" of the knowledge of God and of self into which she withdrew when she resisted the expected course of marriage and motherhood. In her early twenties, she experienced a spiritual vision which moved her to serve the poor and sick, gaining disciples in the process. Catherine was an important defender of the pope as head of the Roman Catholic Church and was canonised in 1461. Saint Catherine is one of the patron saints of Europe and Italy.

Joan of Arc
(c. 1412 - 1431)

Joan of Arc was born into a peasant family in Domrémy, a small village in the northeast of France, during the Hundred Years' War between England and France. As a teenage girl, unable to read or write, she demanded to be taken to the then pre-crowned King Charles VII of France, in 1428 and persuaded him of her divine guidance from God to help him save France from English domination. Unconventionally, she was immediately appointed as a military leader, advising on strategies, providing spiritual leadership, instilling discipline in the troops, and restoring the French army's confidence. She gained recognition as a saviour of France for her role in many military victories, including the liberation of Orléans, which led to the Coronation of Charles VII in 1429. She was captured by Burgundian troops at the Siege of Compiègne in 1430 and burned at the stake by the British on 30th May 1431. Joan of Arc is revered by the French nation as a martyr and is celebrated as an early feminist and a symbol of freedom and independence. In 1920, Joan of Arc was formally canonised by the Roman Catholic Church and officially declared one of the patron saints of France.

Thérèse of Lisieux
(1873 - 1897)

Thérèse of Lisieux, born Marie Françoise-Thérèse Martin, also known as Saint Thérèse of the Child Jesus and the Holy Face, and 'Little Flower of Jesus', entered the Carmelite convent in Lisieux, France at just 15 years old to devote her life to God. Her saintliness came about from her "little ways" approach to spirituality, which has inspired millions of people all over the world to see God's grace in simple tasks and the little things and to trust in God's love. She wrote, "The most trivial work, the least action when inspired by love, is often of greater merit than the most outstanding achievement." She sadly battled with tuberculosis and lived out her final years in quiet reflection, writing her spiritual autobiography, "Story of a Soul", later translated into many languages. The immense popularity of her manuscripts led to her eventual canonisation in 1925, only 28 years after her death. Her sainthood was further elevated in 1947 to the co-protectorship of France alongside Joan of Arc. Thérèse is also the patron saint of florists, orphans and tuberculosis-sufferers.

Florence Li Tim-Oi
(1907 - 1992)

Florence Li Tim-Oi was born in Hong Kong and studied at Canton Union Theological College before going on to become the first woman to be ordained to the priesthood in the Anglican Communion, on 25th January 1944. Anglican means "of England." and stems from British Christians, compelled by the Word of God and the Holy Spirit, to share their faith around the world. During the 'Chinese War of Resistance against Japanese Aggression', from 1937 to 1945, Li was permitted to give the sacraments to Anglicans, a responsibility only bestowed to men by tradition. When the Chinese government closed all churches in China from 1958 to 1974, Li was pressured into working on a farm or in a factory and continued practicing her faith in private. Florence was officially recognised as a priest in the diocese when Hong Kong ordained two further women priests in 1971, and she was appointed an honorary assistant priest in Toronto in 1983, where she spent the remainder of her life.

Wendy Beckett
(1930 - 2018)

Wendy Mary Beckett was a religious sister, author, and art historian who became an unlikely international television celebrity in her later years when she presented a series of art history documentaries. Born in South Africa, and raised in Edinburgh, Scotland, she was just 16 when she entered the Sisters of Notre Dame de Namur, a Roman Catholic congregation founded to provide education to the poor. After graduating with the highest honours in English literature at St Anne's College, Oxford, she returned to South Africa to teach and became the Reverend Mother at a convent in Johannesburg. In 1970, epileptic seizures brought on by stress led her to return to England for a life of prayer and quiet contemplation, residing in a small caravan on the grounds of a Carmelite monastery in Norfolk. There, she translated medieval Latin manuscripts in solitude for many years until deciding to avidly pursue her interest in art. Sister Wendy was 58 when her first book, Contemporary Women Artists, was published, and aged 61 when she debuted as a popular television presenter for the BBC. She continued to present programmes into her early 80s and wrote over 50 books covering the subjects of art, religious icons, and meditations.

Rachel Treweek
(b. 1963)

Rachel Treweek was consecrated as the 41st Bishop of Gloucester in 2015 and made history by becoming the first female bishop in the House of Lords after passing the Lords Spiritual (Women) Act 2015. Rachel believes that God should be considered to be neither male nor female and does her best to avoid using 'he' or 'she' gender-specific pronouns when referring to God. During her time as the Bishop of Gloucester, she has launched two internationally recognised campaigns #Liedentity and Fighting for Women's Justice. The #Liedentity campaign was launched in 2016 and raises awareness of body image anxiety in young people and the pressures they face through social media to look a certain way. With a particular passion for protecting vulnerable girls and women, she launched the campaign Fighting for Women's Justice in 2017. The campaign aims to change the women's justice system and raise awareness of the incredible work that takes place through Women's Centres across the country, supporting the most vulnerable women in our communities.

Libby Lane
(b. 1966)

Elizabeth Jane Holden Lane is a bishop in the Church of England and is one of the Lords Spiritual in the House of Lords. Libby was one of the first cohort of women in the UK to be ordained C of E priests in 1994. Then, following the change in canon law allowing women to become C of E bishops in 2014, Libby was announced as the very first female bishop in the Church of England, when she was consecrated as the Bishop of Stockport at York Minster in 2015. The Rt Rev. Lane was installed to serve as Bishop of Derby and appointed to the House of Lords in 2019. Although female bishops were already present within Anglican churches around the world before this time, the ordination of women remains a contested area. She has said, "I think we are a better organisation for being able to have an honest, robust disagreement that doesn't stop us from serving the kingdom of God together."

About the Author / Illustrator

Diana is an independent author/illustrator from the North of England. She has lived for many years in the beautiful, historic Yorkshire village of Haworth, home to the famous Brontë family during the Victorian era. Taking positive inspiration from her local, strong-willed, female literary legends, and a life-long love of learning and creating art, led to her developing a unique range of hand-illustrated biography/colouring books. 'Herstories' aim to calm, celebrate, and inspire through the mindful practice of colouring.

More 'Herstories' by Diana:

The Brontë Colouring Book
The Great Northern Women Colouring Book
The Great Art Herstory Colouring Book
The Great Scottish Women Colouring Book
The Great Welsh Women Colouring Book
The Great Irish Women Colouring Book
The Great National Health Colouring Book
The Great Business Women Colouring Book